Original title:
Moonlit Frost

Copyright © 2024 Swan Charm
All rights reserved.

Author: Daisy Dewi
ISBN HARDBACK: 978-9916-79-909-3
ISBN PAPERBACK: 978-9916-79-910-9
ISBN EBOOK: 978-9916-79-911-6

Midnight's Icy Breath

The moon hangs low and bright,
Casting shadows in the night.
Whispers of the chilling air,
Silent secrets everywhere.

Frosted whispers kiss my skin,
A touch of magic from within.
Stars above, like diamonds glow,
In the quiet, soft and slow.

The world is wrapped in slumber deep,
While dreams around the night do creep.
Every breath, a cloud of white,
In the heart of frozen night.

Trees stand tall, adorned in lace,
Nature's art, a frozen grace.
Midnight casts its silent spell,
In the stillness, all is well.

I walk the path with steps so light,
Guided by the stars so bright.
In this realm of crystal air,
Midnight's breath, a whispered prayer.

Shimmering Stillness

In the quiet of the dusk,
A world lies still and hushed.
Silver glimmers on the lake,
Nature's heart begins to wake.

Reflections dance on water's face,
A perfect calm, a gentle space.
The sky painted in soft pastel,
In this haven, all is well.

Breezes whisper through the trees,
Carrying tales of memories.
Stars emerge, their light so clear,
In the stillness, night draws near.

Nocturnal creatures start their roam,
In the stillness, far from home.
Underneath the velvet sky,
Shimmering dreams begin to fly.

Each heartbeat in this quiet place,
Finds a rhythm, finds its grace.
In the beauty that surrounds,
Shimmering stillness, peace abounds.

The Night's Glistening Grasp

Night descends with velvet wings,
Holding secrets, lost in strings.
Moonbeams dance on silver streams,
In the dark, we chase our dreams.

Stars igniting the inky sea,
A tapestry of mystery.
Whispers echo through the trees,
Carried gently by the breeze.

Glistening lights from worlds afar,
Guide our hearts like a wishing star.
Embraced by shadows, soft and deep,
In the night's hold, we still keep.

Time stands still, a moment vast,
Every heartbeat, every gasp.
Wrapped in darkness, we find our way,
The night's grasp shall never sway.

In the silence, truths unveil,
Stories woven in a tale.
Life unfolds in shadows cast,
With the night, we breathe steadfast.

Reflections in a Frozen Stream

A mirror lies beneath the ice,
Captured dreams, a paradise.
Reflections swirl in twilight glow,
A tale of time, both fast and slow.

In winter's grasp, the world stands still,
Echoing with a silent thrill.
Each ripple tells of seasons past,
Frozen whispers, memories cast.

Beneath the frost, life breathes anew,
In the heart of winter's hue.
Nature's canvas, painted bright,
Underneath the silver light.

Branches dipped in icy glass,
Moments fleeting, yet they last.
Captured echoes, soft and sweet,
Frozen dreams beneath our feet.

With every step, the world awakes,
Through frozen paths, our journey takes.
In the stillness, life extends,
Reflections true, where beauty blends.

Ephemeral Frosted Dreams

In the silent night, dreams softly bloom,
Frost on petals, caught in moonlight's loom.
Whispers of wishes float on the air,
As time melts gently, beyond all care.

Each moment a glimmer, fleeting yet bright,
Shadows embrace the quiet delight.
Chasing the echoes of yesteryear's gleam,
Within the heart lies an ephemeral dream.

Kisses of the Icy Stars

Stars twinkle high with a frosty embrace,
Icy whispers dance in the celestial space.
Each kiss a promise, a shimmering light,
Guiding our souls through the depths of the night.

A tapestry woven of silver and blue,
Kisses so tender that feel ever new.
In the stillness, the universe sighs,
As dreams take flight, kissed by the skies.

Traces of Celestial Whispers

In the silence, secrets begin to unfold,
Whispers of stardust, adventures untold.
Tracing the paths where the comets have roamed,
In the cosmic ballet, our hearts find a home.

Each whisper a melody, soft and divine,
Echoing softly through the corridors of time.
Floating like shadows on the canvas of night,
Traces of magic that shimmer with light.

Dreamscapes in Silver Shadows

Through silver shadows, the dreamscapes weave,
Crafting illusions that we dare to believe.
Sculpted in starlight, they stretch and entwine,
Whispers of visions where memories shine.

Every echo whispers a tale to explore,
In the depths of the dark, our spirits can soar.
Lost in the patterns of dreams that we chase,
In the dance of the night, we find our place.

The Dance of Glimmering Spirits

In shadows soft they sway,
A leaf-like twirl in the night,
Whispers of dreams alight,
Glimmers of hopes in flight.

Moonbeams brush the ground,
Silent echoes find their way,
Dancing spirits unbound,
In a shimmering ballet.

Stars twinkle in delight,
Guiding each graceful turn,
Painting visions so bright,
As the night softly burns.

With laughter in the air,
They twine in cosmic grace,
Weaving tales so rare,
In this enchanted space.

As dawn breaks the spell,
The spirits drift away,
Leaving a gentle swell,
Of magic's fleeting play.

Secrets Told in Shining Ice

Crystals catch the light,
Whispering secrets old,
Stories of long lost nights,
In a silence so bold.

Frozen tears of time,
Glistening in the sun,
Each shard a rhyme,
Of what once had begun.

Beneath the tranquil sheen,
Echoes softly glide,
Ghosts of places seen,
Where memories abide.

The frost unveils its tale,
With each glimmering breath,
A delicate veil,
Between life and death.

As shadows start to melt,
Revealing warmth beneath,
The secrets gently felt,
In whispers of the wreath.

Halos of Dim Light

In twilight's tender embrace,
Halos form in the haze,
Softly glowing with grace,
Chasing away the maze.

Flickers dance on the wall,
With shadows that entwine,
Silent dreams gently call,
In a world so divine.

Each flicker tells a tale,
Of moments long since past,
When silence wove its veil,
In memories that last.

Underneath the dim glow,
Hearts beat with a rhythm,
In the stillness, we know,
Life's ethereal prism.

As the night wears on slow,
Halos begin to fade,
Yet in us, they will stow,
The light that won't evade.

A Midnight's Frosted Tapestry

Threaded in silver dreams,
A tapestry unfurls,
Whispers of moonlit beams,
With secrets of the swirls.

Each stitch a tale of ice,
Woven with threads of fate,
In patterns soft and nice,
Reflecting moments great.

Stars are stitched with care,
Cradled in winter's breath,
Laced with a fragrant air,
Embroidered tales of death.

As midnight casts its spell,
The tapestry will glow,
With memories to tell,
In the night's gentle flow.

When dawn breaks on the scene,
The frosted art will fade,
Yet in dreams, it will glean,
The beauty that it made.

Ethereal Luminescence Over Snow

In the hush of night, the world aglow,
Whispers of silver, the softest flow.
Blankets of white, a shimmering veil,
Stars winking gently, a luminous trail.

Moonlight dances, a spectral sigh,
Frosted branches reach for the sky.
Magic unfurls in a crystal hue,
Nature's romance, forever true.

Shadows play tricks on the pale ground,
Mysteries hidden where dreams abound.
Every flake glistens, a fleeting grace,
In winter's embrace, a sacred space.

Silvery echoes of a tranquil night,
Every heartbeat a gentle light.
Ethereal whispers in the deep dark,
Shimmering echoes leave their mark.

Through frosted windows, the world looks bright,
An endless canvas, pure and white.
Ethereal luminescence glories above,
A world reborn, wrapped in love.

A Veil of Nighttime Jewels

Cloaked in darkness, the heavens gleam,
A tapestry woven, a starlit dream.
Diamonds glisten on the soft night air,
Each twinkle a promise, beyond compare.

Gentle breezes whisper low,
Crickets sing soft, an evening show.
Moonlight spills like liquid gold,
An ethereal story waiting to be told.

Every gem a memory cast,
In the heart of night, shadows are vast.
A veil drawn tight, yet spirits soar,
In jeweled silence, we crave for more.

Rustling leaves hold secrets of time,
Each moment a rhythm, a perfect rhyme.
Bathed in hues of deep indigo,
The night reveals all we yearn to know.

A stage of wonders, quiet, sublime,
A universe flourished in perfect rhyme.
Beneath the stars, the world finds rest,
In a veil of jewels, we are blessed.

Shivering Brilliance

Glistening frost on the sunrise's crest,
Life's fragile beauty, a treasured guest.
Brushing the surface, a delicate trace,
In every moment, the heart finds grace.

Nature awakens, a gentle sigh,
Vivid hues dance in the blushing sky.
Every shadow a tale to tell,
In the cold embrace, all is well.

Each crystal shard catches the light,
A shivering brilliance in morning bright.
Echoes of laughter, the world anew,
In a tapestry woven of crystal blue.

Chasing the dawn, the chill retreats,
Life springs forth in jubilant beats.
The canvas alive, colors unfold,
Shivering brilliance, a sight to behold.

Golden rays kiss the frosty ground,
A symphony only nature's found.
In every breath, the magic flows,
In shivering brilliance, the heart grows.

Shattered Light on Frozen Ground

Morning breaks upon a crystal sea,
Shattered light dances, wild and free.
Fragments of dawn scatter wide,
In the chill of winter's breath, they glide.

Every ray a whisper of peace,
Promises held in the subtlest crease.
Frozen beauty, a fleeting sight,
Beneath the heavens, day chases night.

With each shard, stories softly gleam,
In the heart of ice, hopes intertwine and dream.
Nature's canvas, painted bright,
Shattered light, a spirit's flight.

As shadows linger, whispers appear,
In frozen moments, the world draws near.
Every sparkle a tale it narrates,
Of winter's heart and the warmth it creates.

Through the stillness, a symphony rings,
Of shattered light and the joy it brings.
On frozen ground, we find our way,
In each glimmer, a brand new day.

Beneath the Midnight Gleam

Stars twinkle softly in the night,
Whispered dreams take eager flight.
Moonlight dances on the ground,
In the silence, magic is found.

Winds of secrets gently sigh,
While shadows weave as time slips by.
Each heartbeat echoes in the dark,
Fueling the fire, igniting a spark.

Beneath the cloak of velvet skies,
Mysteries linger and softly rise.
With every breath, I feel the pull,
The unknown beckons, beautiful, full.

Night's embrace, both calm and wild,
Each moment's treasure, nature's child.
In the depths of stillness, I reflect,
The world outside, vast and circumspect.

Beneath the midnight gleam I stand,
With the cosmos resting in my hand.
Enchanted by the vast display,
I'll follow the stars, come what may.

Ethereal Crystals at Dusk

As daylight wanes and colors blend,
Crystals shimmer, their edges bend.
The horizon blushes, kissed by light,
In this moment, day turns to night.

Glistening jewels on the fading grass,
Whispering tales of the hours that pass.
The sky adorned in shades of gold,
Nature's secrets quietly told.

Each dewdrop a world, reflecting dreams,
As twilight weaves its delicate seams.
Time slows down in the cooling air,
Magic twinkles everywhere.

Birds sing softly, bidding goodbye,
To the sun sinking low in the sky.
With every note, the dusk draws near,
Wrapping the earth in comfort and cheer.

Ethereal whispers of fading light,
Guide us gently into the night.
In this tranquil, serene ballet,
Nature's beauty holds sway.

Frost-kissed Serenade

Morning whispers with icy breath,
Nature lies still, in quiet death.
Frost-kissed leaves shimmer and shine,
A delicate lace, a design divine.

Blankets of white cover the land,
As if the world took a gentle hand.
Each branch adorned with shimmering hues,
A silent symphony of wintry blues.

Footsteps crunch on the frozen ground,
In this serene, perfect, peaceful sound.
The air is crisp, the sky a pearl,
In this frozen moment, dreams unfurl.

Whispers of winter float on by,
As delicate snowflakes waltz and fly.
In every swirl and every fall,
Nature recites her lovely thrall.

Frost-kissed serenade fills the day,
In shimmering breath, the light will play.
Wrapped in beauty, delicate and fair,
Winter's embrace, beyond compare.

Luminous Shadows on Ice

Underneath the moon's bright gaze,
Shadowed figures dance in a daze.
Icy surfaces shimmer and pulse,
Where every movement starts to convulse.

Reflected light, a sparkling dream,
Painting pathways with a silver gleam.
Every glide on the frozen stage,
A fleeting moment, a whispered page.

Beneath the stars, stories are spun,
In the stillness, we all are one.
Each twinkle holds a tale untold,
In luminous shadows, warmth unfolds.

With every breath, the night ignites,
A canvas bright with dazzling lights.
In this ballet, we lose our fears,
With laughter mingled in the chilled air.

Luminous shadows softly trace,
The gentle beauty of this place.
On ice we'll dance 'til morning's light,
Forever bound in winter's night.

Tranquil Frost under Night's Canopy

The moon whispers softly, pale and bright,
Casting shadows that dance with delight.
Stars twinkle above in a velvet sea,
While the world sleeps, wild and free.

Frost kisses leaves, a delicate lace,
Each breath a cloud in this tranquil space.
The night wraps around, a gentle embrace,
Nature's symphony, a cosmic chase.

Silent pines stand tall, guardians of dreams,
As a gentle breeze hums soft, subtle themes.
Crickets chirp tales of the days gone by,
Under the watchful, eternal sky.

In the stillness, the heart finds its beat,
As the world drifts slowly, embracing defeat.
The frost glistens bright in moon's tender gaze,
While the night weaves spells in a silvery haze.

Each moment unfolds like a petal in bloom,
In this tranquil realm, no fear, no gloom.
Wrapped in the frost under night's grand design,
I find peace and solace, a gift divine.

Echoes of a Starry Embrace

In the stillness, whispers travel far,
Carried on winds, they echo a star.
A cosmic dance unfolds in the night,
Cradled by darkness, imbued with light.

Galaxies twirl in a celestial ballet,
Guiding lost souls to where shadows play.
Each twinkling gem tells a tale untold,
Of journeys and dreams, of hearts daring bold.

The silence hums with a radiant tune,
As constellations flicker, a celestial boon.
In the depths of the sky, my spirit takes flight,
Embraced by the warmth of the cool, starry night.

Through the cosmos, I wander and weave,
Lost in the beauty that night helps conceive.
The echoes of love resonate in the dark,
Guiding the dreamers to follow their spark.

With each breath, the universe sings,
Of hopes and of fears, the freedom it brings.
In the tapestry woven from light and from grace,
I find my reflection in this starry embrace.

Glacial Echoes Under Starlight

In the silence, whispers creep,
Underneath the stars so deep.
Ice reflects the night's embrace,
In this stillness, time holds space.

Frozen air, a breath of chill,
Moonlit shadows, soft and still.
Echoes of a distant song,
In the dark where dreams belong.

Snowflakes dance on whispered winds,
Stories of where daylight ends.
Each moment, a fleeting spark,
Glacial echoes in the dark.

Frosted trees in midnight glow,
Carrying secrets of the snow.
In their branches, tales unfold,
Of ancient nights and dreams retold.

Beneath the starlit canopy,
Wonders of eternity.
In the silence, hearts ignite,
Glacial echoes, pure delight.

A Whisper of Gentle Fragrance

Petals scatter on the breeze,
Softly carried through the trees.
A gentle touch, a fleeting kiss,
In the air, a hint of bliss.

Lavender and rose entwine,
Nature's perfume, sweet and fine.
Each breath brings the earth alive,
In this moment, senses thrive.

Morning dew on blades of grass,
As time meanders, hours pass.
With every scent, a memory,
Of a place serene and free.

Whispers of the blooming night,
Fragrance wrapped in soft twilight.
In this world, we find our peace,
Where the fragrant moments cease.

A garden filled with dreams in bloom,
A sweet escape from daily gloom.
In the air, pure magic sways,
A whisper through the sunlit days.

Frigid Radiance in the Night

Cold embraces, starlight's kiss,
In the silence, moments bliss.
Every twinkle, crisp and clear,
Forms a blanket, drawing near.

Ice and light in dance collide,
Over valleys, wild and wide.
Frigid radiance paints the sky,
In its beauty, spirits fly.

Winter's breath in beauty breathes,
Woven low among the leaves.
Each glimmer tells of tales untold,
In its grasp, both warm and cold.

Layers of frost, a glistening hue,
Underneath the midnight blue.
In this wonder, hearts align,
Frigid radiance, so divine.

Moments wrapped in shimmering light,
In the depth of winter's night.
Nature whispers, soft and bright,
Frigid beauty, pure delight.

Glimmering Veil of the Cosmos

In the sky, a hidden grace,
Stars appear, a twinkling face.
The cosmos wears a glimmering veil,
Tales of time and dreams set sail.

Nebulae in colors spread,
Whispers of the dreams we've bred.
Galaxies swirl, twirl in flight,
Dancing 'neath the endless night.

Stardust clouds of silver gleam,
As we wander through the dream.
Each angle, light in perfect form,
In its embrace, we feel the warm.

Celestial paths fade and gleam,
Eternal patterns in the stream.
The universe sings soft and slow,
In its rhythm, hearts will glow.

Infinite realms, a wondrous sight,
Captured in the velvet night.
A glimmering veil to explore,
In the cosmos, forevermore.

Radiant Illusions on Frozen Rivers

A silver sheen on ice so bright,
Reflections dance in pale moonlight.
Whispers float on chilly air,
Echoes of dreams, both bold and rare.

Stillness holds the world in thrall,
As shadows stretch, the night does call.
Beneath the surface secrets lie,
Silent tales of days gone by.

Stars twinkle like frozen tears,
Beneath the frost, a world appears.
In this realm where time stands still,
Magic brews in winter's chill.

Gliding softly, spirits roam,
On frozen paths, they call it home.
Radiant visions, bright and clear,
Embracing all that we hold dear.

With every step upon the ice,
Nature's canvas, a grand device.
Illusions sparkle, dreams arise,
In this realm beneath the skies.

Dreams Entwined in Winter's Glow

In the hush of a frozen night,
Dreams weave softly, a gentle sight.
Warmth in whispers, touch of fate,
Embers glow as hearts create.

Snowflakes drift like thoughts unchained,
Each one unique, delicately stained.
A tapestry of silver light,
Where wishes soar and spirits ignite.

Stars above, like candles bright,
Guide the way through winter's night.
Paths converge in quiet grace,
In this stillness, find our place.

Hands entwined, we chase the glow,
In every heartbeat, warmth will flow.
Together, lost in frosty airs,
Through dreams we wander, unawares.

In the cold, our spirits rise,
Wrapped in visions, love never dies.
As morning breaks, dawn's soft embrace,
In winter's glow, we find our trace.

Illuminated Silhouettes in Hazy Nights

Figures dance in dim-lit haze,
Casting shadows in delicate ways.
Softly spoken secrets shared,
In dim corners, hearts laid bare.

Streetlamps flicker, a warm embrace,
Fleeting moments time cannot erase.
Whispers echo through the air,
Silent stories that we all share.

Faces fade in the amber light,
Lost in reverie, they take flight.
Underneath the starry dome,
Illuminated, we feel at home.

Night unveils a silent grace,
Holding dreams in its gentle space.
As the world spins, we find our song,
In these silhouettes, we belong.

Hazy visions, a world surreal,
In the darkness, we learn to feel.
United in this soft embrace,
Illuminated, we find our place.

Crystal Veils that Shimmer

Through branches draped in frosty lace,
Crystal veils that time can't erase.
Sunlight kisses every shard,
Nature's jewels, exquisite, hard.

Glistening paths where fairies tread,
Whispers of magic, softly spread.
In every spark, a story lies,
Caught within winter's crystal sighs.

Each step taken, pure delight,
In this realm, everything feels right.
A tapestry of glimmering dreams,
Flowing gently in winter streams.

Awakening senses with each breath,
In this wonder, defying death.
A dance of life in chilly air,
Crystal veils that we lovingly share.

Beauty clings to every tree,
In this world, where hearts roam free.
Beneath the shimmer, we will find,
The threads of magic that bind mankind.

Night's Crystal Waltz

The moonlight drapes the silent ground,
With shadows dancing all around.
Each whisper of the evening breeze,
Carries dreams with gentle ease.

Stars twinkle like a lover's gaze,
In the magic of the night's embrace.
The world slows down, a soft refrain,
In this waltz of joy and pain.

Silver frost on window sills,
Reflects the quiet of the hills.
A symphony of twinkling lights,
Weaving tales of starry nights.

The trees sway gently, lit so bright,
In the hush of the velvet night.
Lost in the beauty of the trance,
We surrender to the moon's dance.

In this moment, time stands still,
Embraced by the night, our hearts will fill.
Together under cosmic skies,
We find our truth in lonesome sighs.

Breath of the Glacial Silence

Winter's breath awakens the scene,
Crystals forming where the grass has been.
A soft hush blankets all around,
In the stillness, peace is found.

Frosted leaves in a slumber deep,
Guard secrets that the night will keep.
An echo of the ancient cold,
Speaks in whispers, stories told.

Moonlight dances on icy streams,
Reflecting the world of silver dreams.
Branches bow with a heavy weight,
As if burdened by fate.

In the heart of the frozen wood,
Silent echoes speak of good.
The world awakens, breathes anew,
In this glacial silence, pure and true.

A moment captured, serene, divine,
In the stillness, our spirits entwine.
Nature's heartbeat, gentle and light,
Guides us through the frosty night.

Glistening Awakenings Under Starlight

As dawn breaks, the stars start to fade,
Awakening dreams that night had laid.
With soft blush of the morning skies,
A dance unfolds, where beauty lies.

Glistening dew on petals bright,
Reflects the remnants of the night.
Whispers of hope in the soft glow,
As the world greets the sun's warm show.

Songs of birds in joyful cheer,
Fill the air, inviting near.
A gentle breeze, a tender touch,
Reminds us why we love so much.

Under starlight, we took a chance,
The universe held our fleeting glance.
In every shimmer, a story found,
Hearts entwined as magic bound.

The day awakens, alive and free,
In nature's beauty, just you and me.
We greet the morning with sweet delight,
In glistening awakenings, pure and bright.

Frosty Glimmering Reveries

In the quiet of a winter's dawn,
Frosted breath lingers, lightly drawn.
Nature glimmers in icy attire,
A world transformed, glowing like fire.

Crystal lace weaves through the trees,
Whispers of winter carried by the breeze.
Each flake a wish, a soft caress,
In frost, we find a gentle dress.

The pale sun rises, light so rare,
Illuminating the frosty air.
In the hush, a magic unfolds,
A tapestry of dreams and golds.

Footsteps crunch on the frozen ground,
In the stillness, a heartbeat found.
Our thoughts take flight, like snowflakes spun,
In frosty reveries, we become one.

As day breaks clear, we hold the light,
In glimmering beauty, hearts ignite.
Embracing winter's soft embrace,
In this frozen world, we find our place.

Whispers of Silver Chill

In shadows deep, the night unfolds,
A breath of frost, the silence holds.
A gentle sigh of winter's breath,
Where dreams and whispers dance with death.

Soft silver glimmers on the ground,
Each step a whisper, barely found.
The world adorned in sapphire light,
Embraced by peace, the heart takes flight.

A cadence sweet, the moonlight sings,
Through frosted boughs and shivering wings.
Echoes linger, softly trace,
The chill upon the smiling face.

In twilight's arms, the stillness grows,
Where tales of ice and beauty flows.
A longing wraps like winter's shawl,
As silver whispers beckon all.

A Veil of Ice and Dream

A curtain drawn of crystal clear,
The world beneath, a realm sincere.
In dreams of ice, we softly glide,
Through gentle fog, where hopes reside.

Each flake a wish, a tender thought,
In silence dressed, ethereal caught.
The moon imbues the night with grace,
As dreams and echoes interlace.

A tranquil hush, the heart does race,
As shadows dance, a slow embrace.
A mirror bright of frosted sky,
In icy realms, our spirits fly.

With every breath, the stillness hums,
A harmony that gently thrums.
Veiled in ice, our spirits beam,
Awakening on the edge of dream.

Night's Glimmering Touch

Upon the edge of night's soft veil,
A touch of light, a whispered tale.
With stars that twinkle, hearts are stirred,
In shadowed realms, where dreams are blurred.

Each glimmer bright, a spark of hope,
In darkened skies, we learn to cope.
The night unveils its cosmic charm,
Embracing souls with gentle warmth.

A silver thread weaves through the dark,
Illuminating every spark.
In twilight's hug, the world awaits,
As moonlight graces silver fates.

A serenade of stars above,
Whispers of peace, a song of love.
In night's embrace, our fears take flight,
With glimmering touch, we greet the night.

Celestial Crystals at Dusk

As daylight fades, the sky ignites,
In hues of gold, where sparkle bites.
Celestial crystals, bright and rare,
Dress twilight's cloak with utmost care.

Each gem a story from afar,
Reflecting dreams, both near and far.
They dance like fireflies through the dusk,
A shimmering glow, a fragrant musk.

In twilight's arms, the world stands still,
With every glance, our hearts do thrill.
An echo of the day's last light,
As stars emerge, twinkling bright.

Beneath the dome of navy blue,
Crystals shimmer with a hue.
At dusk's sweet edge, we find our way,
In hope's embrace, we softly sway.

Twilight's Silvery Lace

The sun dips low, a fading light,
Casting shadows, whispering night.
Stars peep out, a twinkling grace,
Wrapped in the hush of twilight's lace.

Soft breezes sway the trees so tall,
Nature sings a quiet call.
Moonlit paths where dreamers trace,
Lost in the beauty, time can't erase.

Crickets chirp their evening songs,
While darkened skies where silence throngs.
A world transformed in gentle space,
Carved from dreams with silver lace.

Glimmers dance on the shallow brook,
Inviting hearts to stop and look.
In this moment, find solace's place,
Embracing peace, like twilight's grace.

Whispers of Silver Chill

The night creeps in with a silver chill,
Moonlight drapes the world so still.
Whispers float on the icy breeze,
Carried soft through the darkened trees.

Frosted leaves in the muted glow,
Nature bathes in a tender flow.
Every shadow, a secret to reveal,
In the embrace of the silver chill.

Stars spin tales in celestial dance,
Inviting hearts to take a chance.
A world awash in the night's surreal,
Where dreams unfold in whispers, real.

Winter's breath paints a canvas bright,
Magic wrapped in the folds of night.
Harmony sings as we all feel,
The soft caress of the silver chill.

Dance of the Glowing Shards

Across the sky, where dreams align,
Fragments spark, a ballet divine.
Stars leap forth, a radiant hue,
In cosmic waltz, both old and new.

Glowing shards ignite the dark,
Each flicker holds a lover's spark.
A dance of fate, in cosmic time,
Celestial rhythms, pure and prime.

Silk of night, a soft embrace,
Welcomes souls to join the chase.
Through ethereal paths, we glide and glide,
With hearts ablaze, in this starry ride.

Echoes of laughter swirl in the air,
In this sacred space, we dare.
With eyes closed tight, we lose our guard,
In the dance of the glowing shards.

The Elegy of Soft Shadows

In twilight's grasp, shadows wane,
Whispers echo, soft, in vain.
A requiem for what is lost,
Memories linger, counting cost.

Beneath the trees, sighs intertwine,
Time drips slowly, like aged wine.
A dance of silhouettes in flight,
Fading softly into night.

The moonlight bathes the earth in gold,
Tales of the brave and the bold.
Yet in the quiet, hearts do ache,
For each shadow, a bond to break.

Cloaked in dreams, the past takes root,
In every corner, a ghostly pursuit.
But in the stillness, hope remains,
Elevating love through endless pains.

With every dusk, we find the grace,
To cherish shadows we can't replace.
An elegy, tender, bittersweet,
For soft shadows, where heartbeats meet.

Whispering Haze of the Night

In the hush, secrets float and weave,
Moonlit fog, a soft reprieve.
Stars invite the dreams to soar,
Whispers linger, wanting more.

The night unfolds with tender grace,
Each sigh wraps the world in lace.
Hazy visions gently blend,
A melody that knows no end.

Through branches thick, the shadows play,
Casting doubts around their sway.
Yet in this shroud of sweet allure,
The heart finds solace, still and pure.

Laughter dances in the air,
Echoes of joy, a lover's stare.
In every pulse, a secret song,
In every note, where dreams belong.

As dawn approaches, dreams take flight,
With every breath, a soft goodnight.
The haze now fades with day's bright cheer,
But whispers linger, ever near.

The Silent Call of the Ice

Beneath the frost, a world in hush,
Silent glints of light that rush.
Crystal shards that gleam and shine,
Each breath whispers of the divine.

Frozen lands stretch far and wide,
Whispers of winter cannot hide.
Nature sleeps, yet dreams awake,
In the stillness, hearts will ache.

The frozen veil, a somber cloak,
Each crack a tale, softly spoke.
And in the silence, nature's thrall,
A haunting echo of winter's call.

Icicles drip like fleeting time,
Every drop a fleeting rhyme.
In cold embrace, we find our place,
In pure stillness, the heart can race.

As seasons change and ice will melt,
The silent call is deeply felt.
Yet from the frost, warmth will arise,
To lift the soul toward bright skies.

Enigma of the Chilled Dreamscape

In realms of frost, where shadows dance,
Dreams collide with a fleeting glance.
Chilled whispers float on tendrils fine,
In a dreamscape where stars align.

Veils of mist on the moon's embrace,
Every step, a softened trace.
Echoes linger in the stillness deep,
Woven tales the night will keep.

Frosted petals, fragile bloom,
In the hush, they chase the gloom.
Yet in the cool, warmth starts to creep,
A promise born from midnight's sleep.

Through veils of ice, the mind will roam,
Searching for a whispered home.
Each corner turned, a shadowy fright,
In the enigma of the night.

Awake to find the sweetness fades,
As dawn dissolves the chilling shades.
Yet in our hearts, the dream remains,
A timeless echo, love's refrains.

Crystals of Midnight Harmony

Under the veil of starlit dreams,
Crystals sing soft melodies,
Whispers of night in moonlit beams,
Bringing peace like gentle seas.

Each sparkle twinkles like the heart,
Mapping trails of silver light,
In this stillness, we won't part,
Embracing shadows, holding tight.

Beneath the dome of velvet skies,
Echoes dance with every breeze,
In crystal worlds, our spirits rise,
Lost in timeless reveries.

Nature breathes in harmony,
Brewing magic through the air,
In the calm, we find the key,
A bond that whispers everywhere.

Together in the midnight glow,
Crystals hum of love's refrain,
In this enchanted night's flow,
We find solace in the rain.

Luminary of the Frigid Sky

A beacon bright in frosty air,
Guiding lost souls from afar,
With gentle glimmers, soft and rare,
The cosmos speaks through each star.

In silence deep, the night unfolds,
Blanketing Earth in icy peace,
The luminary gently holds,
Whispers of hope that never cease.

Navigating through the stark cold,
Gleaming paths for dreams to chase,
Stories of warmth and hearts unrolled,
In the vastness of time and space.

As shadows stretch and hearts align,
We dance beneath that frosty glow,
In every twinkle, love's design,
Binding us in the cosmic flow.

Underneath the shimmering night,
A promise whispers in the chill,
Together we soar, hearts ignite,
In the quiet, our dreams fulfill.

Frosted Twilight Reveries

When dusk descends in frosted hues,
The world is draped in silver mist,
Captured moments we could choose,
In twilight's embrace, none are missed.

Shadows dance with whispers low,
Painting tales on twilight's skin,
In this soft light, our spirits flow,
Reveries born, where dreams begin.

Frosted petals gently fall,
Kissing earth with each caress,
In nature's breath, we hear the call,
A lullaby of sweet finesse.

As silver stars awaken life,
We cradle hopes in quiet night,
Casting aside worry and strife,
Finding warmth in shared light.

Together we weave visions bright,
In every pause, a promise glows,
Through frosted dreams, our hearts take flight,
In twilight's dance, love freely flows.

In the Hush of Glimmering Night

In the hush of night so deep,
Glimmers weave a tapestry,
Calling whispers from their sleep,
Lending grace to mystery.

Stars ignite in cosmic dance,
Silencing the world below,
In this moment, we take chance,
To discover all we know.

Shadows stretch and softly sigh,
Embracing dreams that dare to soar,
In this magic, you and I,
Find the keys to every door.

With each breath, the night unfolds,
Stories whispered through the breeze,
In glimmering hues, our hearts behold,
A future painted with such ease.

Together, we share the light,
In the hush, two souls unite,
Cradled in the peaceful night,
We find our way, forever bright.

Radiance on a Glacial Canvas

Awash in hues of softest light,
Icicles shimmer, crystal bright.
Each beam reflects on frozen ground,
In silence, beauty's warmth is found.

Veils of mist weave through the trees,
Whispers carried on the breeze.
A tapestry of ice and sun,
Nature's art, forever spun.

Colors blend in tranquil grace,
Dancing shadows interlace.
The world awakes from winter's dream,
As daylight paints a vibrant scheme.

Footsteps crunch on frosty trails,
Softly echoing winter's tales.
Amidst the chill, a glow so rare,
Shows us warmth can linger there.

A glacial canvas, pure and vast,
Where every moment holds the past.
In the stillness, hearts take flight,
Embraced by radiance and light.

Frost's Ethereal Embrace

In morning light, the frost does glint,
A delicate touch, soft as a hint.
Nature's breath, a diamond sheen,
Stills the world, a peaceful scene.

Branches bowed with icy lace,
Nature's art in slow embrace.
Whispers of winter, cool and clear,
Hold us close, draw us near.

The air is crisp, a gentle bite,
Yet warmth remains in soft twilight.
In every flake, a story lives,
Of frost that dreams and quietly gives.

Eclipsed by day, the stars now twinkle,
Frosted grass where shadows sprinkle.
In this realm where silence sings,
Winter's charm and peace it brings.

Awash in white, the world transforms,
Embracing chill, where beauty warms.
In frosty breath, we find a space,
Wrapped within its soft embrace.

Illumination in the Quiet

When dusk descends, the world stands still,
As whispers weave through evening chill.
Each star ignites a distant spark,
Illumination in the dark.

The moon spills silver on the ground,
Where shadows whisper, dreams are found.
A tranquil glow, serene and bright,
Guides the heart through velvety night.

Thoughts drift softly, like the breeze,
Carried on whispers through the trees.
In the stillness, hope ignites,
Filling the void with gentle lights.

The world, a canvas, dark yet deep,
Where secrets dwell, and sorrows sleep.
In quiet moments, peace arrives,
Illumination softly thrives.

Each breath a promise, each heartbeat clear,
In this sacred space, draw near.
Amidst the silence, dreams take flight,
Bathed in love, in soft moonlight.

Shadows Dance in the Chill

In twilight hues, the shadows play,
Dancing 'neath the fading day.
The air is crisp, alive with thrill,
As night unfolds, the world is still.

Flickering lights in the deepening night,
Echoing whispers of sheer delight.
Every movement, a gentle sway,
As shadows weave in a ghostly ballet.

Freeze in time, the moment's grace,
In stillness, find a secret place.
Where laughter mingles with the chill,
And dreams awaken, life's yet fulfilled.

The moon casts spells on silvered ground,
A symphony of silence, profound.
Each heartbeat matches the soft refrain,
Of shadows dancing in the rain.

With every twirl, the spirit soars,
As night embraces, the heart explores.
In the chill, a warmth ignites,
In shadows dancing, pure delights.

When Stars Embrace the Cold

Beneath the velvet night sky,
The stars begin to gleam bright,
Whispers of the winter air,
Embrace the silence of the light.

Each twinkle tells a story sweet,
Of frozen dreams and snowy trails,
A dance of wonders overhead,
Where darkness glides, and magic sails.

With every flicker, hearts ignite,
As midnight's breath caresses skin,
In the stillness, hope takes flight,
And warmth emerges from within.

The chilly winds may weave their spell,
Yet starlit paths are ours to tread,
In the cold, our spirits swell,
As cosmic threads are gently spread.

Together under cosmic dome,
We find our solace in this night,
When stars embrace the earth's cool breath,
And fill the world with pure delight.

Frosted Serenade

In the hush of winter's breath,
A melody softly weaves,
Frost kissed notes dance through the air,
As nature quietly believes.

Crystalline whispers play their tune,
On branches glazed with twinkling ice,
Each sound a spark of shimmering light,
In a world so calm and precise.

Ode to the silence that surrounds,
With every flake a whispered song,
The heart of winter pulses strong,
In this embrace where we belong.

Voices of snowflakes softly blend,
Creating harmonies divine,
In this frosted serenade,
Echos of joy forever shine.

As night unfurls its silver veil,
The world becomes a canvas bright,
Every breath a frosted tale,
As stars illuminate the night.

Luminescence in the Stillness

In the shadows, where calm resides,
A gentle glow begins to rise,
Luminescent whispers break
The silence wrapped in velvet skies.

Each flicker, a soft guiding light,
In stillness found beneath the stars,
Colors paint the icy ground,
As night reveals its hidden bars.

The moon sings softly to the dark,
Illuminating frost-kissed trees,
In this quiet, magic sparks,
As spirits dance on frosty breeze.

Through the hush, dreams take their flight,
In a world where shadows play,
Luminescence graces every sight,
And night unfolds in grand display.

We wander through this tranquil space,
Where light and dark harmonize,
In the stillness, we embrace,
The warmth of hope within the skies.

Shadows of the Glacial Night

Beneath the cloak of glacial dreams,
Shadows dance with whispered grace,
In the night where stillness gleams,
A serene and untouched place.

Frosted edges trace the ground,
As worlds collide in hushed delight,
Silent echoes all around,
In the shadows of the night.

Each breath a swirl of silver mist,
As stars peek through the crystal veil,
Glimmers of magic softly kissed,
As whispers of the past unveil.

Frozen tales of ages gone,
Drift upon the air so pure,
In this night, we linger on,
And find our hearts begin to cure.

With every moment, shadows sigh,
In glacial stillness, time holds tight,
Embracing dreams as days go by,
In shadows of the glacial night.

Enchantment Beneath the Stars

Beneath the velvet sky we lie,
Whispers of dreams, a soft sigh.
Constellations twinkle bright,
Guiding our hearts through the night.

In each flicker, magic glows,
Stories of love, the world knows.
Time dances slow, a gentle trance,
Two souls entwined in a cosmic dance.

The moon casts silver on our skin,
A quiet promise, where we begin.
Hand in hand, we drift afar,
Enchanted under the evening star.

Soft breeze carries a secret tune,
Cradling us close, till the dawn in June.
In that moment, all is clear,
With you beside me, I have no fear.

As dawn breaks, the stars fade away,
Yet in our hearts, they always stay.
For every night, a new encore,
Beneath the stars, we'll dream once more.

Frosty Vows in the Twilight

The twilight glimmers, soft and pale,
Covered in frost, the whispers trail.
We stand together, hand in hand,
Making vows upon this frozen land.

Shimmering crystals adorn the trees,
With every promise, carried by the breeze.
Warmth surrounds us, despite the chill,
Two hearts united, stronger still.

Snowflakes dance like fleeting dreams,
In this winter wonder, love redeems.
With every breath, mist fills the air,
In frosty vows, our hearts laid bare.

As darkness deepens, stars emerge bright,
Each one a witness of our delight.
In this stillness, our hearts ignite,
Frosty vows in the fading light.

Together we face the night's embrace,
Finding solace in this sacred space.
Through every snow, and every storm,
Our love endures, forever warm.

Ethereal Echoes of Winter

In wintry woods, silence falls deep,
Where shadows whisper, secrets keep.
Ethereal echoes, a haunting song,
Guiding our footsteps as we wander along.

Moonlight dances on the icy stream,
Frost-kissed branches, a wandering dream.
Every rustle, a tale to tell,
Of love and longing, where we fell.

Veils of snow blanket the ground,
In this stillness, magic is found.
Footprints linger in the glistening white,
In the soft glow of the starry light.

The chill wraps gently around our skin,
A hush envelops, inviting us in.
In whispers low, our spirits rise,
Ethereal echoes under deepening skies.

Winter's breath carries tales anew,
In every sigh, in every hue.
Through frigid nights and dawns of gold,
In ethereal echoes, our love unfolds.

Dance of the Crystal Ghosts

Upon the lake, the moonlight gleams,
Painting the water with silver dreams.
Crystal ghosts in swirling flight,
Whirling softly through the night.

With gentle grace, they weave and spin,
A ghostly waltz, where we begin.
In their shimmer, our stories blend,
A dance eternal, hearts transcend.

Veils of fog rise, while shadows roam,
Here in this place, we find our home.
Through every leap, the whispers sigh,
As echoes of love refuse to die.

With every step, the world feels new,
Crystal spirits, guiding us through.
Under the starlit canvas wide,
In this dance, our souls abide.

As night gives way to day's embrace,
The crystal ghosts leave not a trace.
Yet in our hearts their music stays,
In a dance of love that never sways.

Celestial Shine on Frigid Ground

Stars flicker in the dark,
Their light a gentle hymn.
Whispers of the cosmos,
Caressing fragile skin.

Moonlight spills like silk,
A dance on icy streams.
Nature holds its breath,
Wrapped within night's dreams.

The world, a crystal sphere,
Glistens under clear skies.
Each twinkle a promise,
A spark that never dies.

In the silence of night,
Hope floats on chilly air.
Celestial glow shines bright,
Erasing every care.

On frosted ground we stand,
Beneath the vast expanse.
The night, a hand in hand,
With time, we take our chance.

Glistening Dreams Beneath Stars

In the realm of night's tide,
Dreams shimmer and unfold.
Each star a gleaming guide,
Stories waiting to be told.

Soft whispers on the breeze,
Echoes of distant past.
We dance among the trees,
Moments woven to last.

Glistening hopes take flight,
Carried on playful winds.
Beneath the endless night,
Heartbeats and joy rescinds.

Moonbeams paint the earth bright,
A canvas of silver light.
In dreams, we find our sight,
Sailing through tranquil night.

Awakening with a sigh,
Morning whispers nearby.
But in dreams, we still fly,
Beneath a starlit sky.

Frosted Lullabies

In the stillness of night,
Frosted whispers arise.
Nature sings soft lullabies,
Under gentle moonrise.

Snowflakes dance like whispers,
On chilly breaths of air.
Each flake a tiny dream,
Caught in winter's care.

Crickets hush their songs,
As the world turns to sleep.
Wrapped in frosted throngs,
Promises we shall keep.

Stars twinkle like secrets,
In the velvet night sky.
Guiding our hopes and wishes,
As we close our eyes.

With every frozen breeze,
Comfort lingers near.
Frosted lullabies tease,
Whispering sweet cheer.

A Silvered Night's Embrace

In silver's soft embrace,
Night whispers gentle grace.
Beneath a blanket dark,
Each shadow leaves a mark.

Dreams weave through midnight air,
Carried by silent prayer.
Stars flicker in the deep,
Guarding secrets we keep.

Cold winds brush past my face,
Nature's slow, tender pace.
Moonlight drapes the land bright,
Bathing us in its light.

Thoughts drift like silver threads,
Guiding hearts where hope spreads.
In this night's timeless hold,
Our stories yet untold.

As dawn begins to rise,
Casting hues across skies,
We cherish the night's gift,
As dreams begin to lift.

Fragments of Light in the Dark

In the quiet spaces, shadows creep,
Whispers of hope in silence seep.
Flickers of warmth, a soft glow near,
Guiding lost souls through the night clear.

Stars twinkle gently, a distant song,
Carrying dreams where hearts belong.
Each fragment glimmers, a beacon bright,
Illuminating paths in the darkest night.

Memories dance like fireflies fly,
Through tangled thoughts that drift and sigh.
Holding the glimmers in tender hands,
We weave together our life's demands.

In the stillness, courage blooms wide,
Fragments of light like a soothing tide.
Breaking the silence, a symphony swells,
In every heartbeat, a tale that tells.

As dawn approaches, shadows fade,
In the warmth of light, new hopes are made.
From fragments gathered, we rise anew,
Embracing the day, a world in view.

Nature's Glittering Silence

Beneath the canopy, a stillness reigns,
Whispers of nature, gentle refrains.
Leaves softly rustle, a secret shared,
In this quiet realm, all hearts bared.

Moonlight dances on tranquil streams,
Casting silver dreams in midnight beams.
Crickets serenade, their songs so sweet,
Nature's symphony, pure and complete.

Petals unfold with morning's sigh,
Jewels of dew like stars in the sky.
A tapestry woven from nature's grace,
In glittering silence, we find our place.

Mountains stand tall, steadfast and grand,
Guardians of wisdom, forever they stand.
In every corner, wonders ignite,
Nature's embrace, a pure delight.

As day yields to evening's soft glow,
The world is wrapped in a peaceful flow.
In nature's glitter, we lose all fright,
Finding our solace in the night.

Reflections in Winter's Embrace

Snowflakes descend like whispered thoughts,
Covering the earth in soft, white knots.
Stillness lingers where shadows play,
Winter's embrace greets the fading day.

Frozen rivers, mirrors of glass,
Capture moments as the world will pass.
Each breath a cloud in the cold, crisp air,
A dance of quiet in the frosty glare.

Evergreens stand in their winter coats,
Guarding the dreams that the silence wrote.
Nature pauses, holding her breath,
In reflections deep, we ponder death.

Amidst the stillness, warmth does bloom,
A flicker of hope dispels the gloom.
With every twinkle of stars at night,
Winter's embrace brings new insight.

As seasons turn and time flows on,
We find our strength when winter's gone.
In every flake that falls and glows,
Reflections of life and love we chose.

Crystal Visions by Night

Under the veil of a velvet sky,
Stars emerge as dreams drift by.
Each twinkle a tale of distant lands,
Whispers of magic in nighttime strands.

Moonbeams weave through trees so tall,
Casting shadows that gently fall.
In crystal visions, the world awakes,
A symphony of wonder that never breaks.

Night blossoms like a midnight flower,
Filling the air with tranquil power.
Dreamers roam where silence dwells,
In the whispers of night, their story tells.

Mirrored lakes reflect the skies,
Night's artistry, a sweet surprise.
In each ripple, a sparkle bright,
Guiding lost souls through the moonlit night.

With dawn approaching, visions will fade,
Yet memories linger, a sweet cascade.
In crystal light, we find our way,
Carried by dreams into the day.

A Bed of Stars Cradled in Ice

A blanket of white covers the ground,
Twinkling above, the stars are found.
Whispers of night in the stillness speak,
Cradled in dreams, we drift into sleep.

Silver beams dance on the icy crest,
Nature's beauty wears a frosty vest.
Heartbeats blend with the whispers of cold,
Stories of winter in silence unfold.

Beneath the vast sky, serenity reigns,
Each flake of snow, like joy, remains.
Footprints mark a path through the glade,
While shadows and light weave an endless braid.

In the stillness, a gentle sigh,
As constellations twinkle high.
With each breath, the world feels so vast,
In the silence of night, we find our past.

Wrapped in warmth, the night does embrace,
A bed of stars in this frozen place.
With dreams that soar like the moon above,
We dance in the night, embraced by love.

Sparkling Dreams of a Frozen Night

Under the silver of a moonlit sky,
Dreams take flight, like birds that fly.
Each flake of snow, a wish gently made,
Sparkling bright in the cool night's parade.

Gentle whispers through branches sway,
As frost weaves tales that softly play.
In the hush of night, stories unfold,
Mysteries wrapped in glimmers of gold.

Stars like lanterns guide us near,
Filling our hearts with winter's cheer.
Every breath we take is a soft glow,
In the night where the dreams freely flow.

With a touch of grace, the cosmos begins,
Igniting the magic where silence spins.
Frozen wonders sparkle and gleam,
In this incredible, enchanted dream.

Cradled in night's soft embrace,
We find our solace in this sacred space.
With every heartbeat, let our hopes ignite,
In sparkling dreams of a frozen night.

Celestial Layers of Frost

Layer by layer, the frost does creep,
Blanketing the earth in a slumber deep.
Celestial whispers ride the chill air,
Echoing secrets only night can share.

From the depths of shadows, the stars arise,
Casting their glimmers across the skies.
Each twinkle a promise, each flicker a tale,
In the canvas of night, where wonders prevail.

Icy patterns on glass paint a scene,
Of magic and mystery, soft and serene.
In the silence, the world holds its breath,
Wrapped in the beauty of winter's caress.

Drifting thoughts on a cool, crisp breeze,
Carrying echoes of ancient trees.
In frost-kissed dreams, we find our way,
Through celestial layers, night turns to day.

With every moment, a new vision springs,
In frosty realms, the heart gently sings.
Layers of wonder encompass the night,
In celestial frost, where all feels right.

Mystic Glow After Twilight

As twilight fades, a glow takes flight,
Whispers of magic paint the night.
Stars awaken with a soft, warm gleam,
Creating a tapestry, a vibrant dream.

A hush envelops the tranquil skies,
While shadows dance where the mystery lies.
In the stillness, we feel the embrace,
Of the otherworldly, a gentle grace.

Emerging light in hues of blue,
Carries the secrets of the night anew.
Moonbeams cascade like silk on the ground,
In the mystic glow, peace can be found.

Each flicker of light tells a story untold,
Of wandering souls and hearts brave and bold.
In the afterglow, the world seems to pause,
To witness the beauty without a cause.

With dreams that shimmer in twilight's embrace,
We journey through realms of this tranquil space.
In the whisper of night, our spirits unite,
Under the mystic glow after twilight.

Nocturnal Shimmer

Under the velvet sky, stars gleam,
Whispers of night, a tranquil dream.
Moonlight drapes the earth in lace,
Silent shadows begin to chase.

Crickets sing their midnight song,
In the dark, where we belong.
Winds carry tales from afar,
Guided by the light of a star.

Dewdrops glisten, diamonds bright,
Nature sways in soft moonlight.
The world breathes in peaceful sighs,
Beneath the watchful, glowing skies.

The Night's Radiant Veil

Veil of night, so softly spun,
Cradling dreams till day is done.
Stars like jewels, bold yet meek,
Glisten gently, silence speaks.

A hush falls over hill and glade,
In the dusk, all fears allayed.
The milky way flows, shimmering bright,
A ribbon of hope in deepening night.

Whispers of magic fill the air,
A tender dance, a solemn prayer.
Embrace the dark, let shadows play,
For in this realm, the heart finds sway.

Secrets in the Hoarfrost

Morning's breath on the meadow lies,
Hoarfrost glistens under pale skies.
Each flake a secret, a story untold,
Wrapped in silence, shimmering gold.

As sunlight breaks, the chill retreats,
Frosty whispers, enigmatic feats.
Nature's canvas, a fleeting art,
Glimmers quietly, tugging at the heart.

Every glitter, a memory bright,
Dances softly, fading in light.
Reflecting moments, whispers in time,
Fleeting beauty, a quiet rhyme.

A Chorus of Winter's Light

Winter calls in a gentle tone,
A symphony, in stillness grown.
Snowflakes fall like notes from above,
Each flurry sings of peace and love.

The world adorned in white and gray,
Nature pauses, holds sway.
Frosty air, a crisp delight,
Hearts aglow in the soft twilight.

Beneath the branches, shadows play,
Glistening hope, a bright ballet.
Wrap us in warmth, the fire's embrace,
As winter's light reveals its grace.

The Chill Embrace of Night

The stars whisper softly, high in the sky,
A blanket of darkness, where secrets lie.
Moonlight dances gently on a silver lake,
In the stillness of night, the heart starts to wake.

Shadows stretch long, as the world holds its breath,
In the chill of the air, there's a promise of depth.
Cool winds caress, like a lover's sweet sigh,
Wrapped in night's arms, we begin to fly.

Crickets serenade in a melodic tune,
The hush of the world, beneath the full moon.
Every heartbeat echoes in this serene space,
In the chill embrace, we find our own pace.

Dreams take their flight on the wings of the breeze,
Guiding us softly through the tall, swaying trees.
As the darkness deepens, we venture and roam,
In the arms of the night, we've finally found home.

The clock softly ticks, counting moments so deep,
In the arms of the night, wrapped in silence, we sleep.
Tomorrow will come, with its light and its sound,
But for now, in this chill, our solace is found.

Frosted Fantasies Awakening

The dawn breaks slowly, with a shimmer so fine,
Dew on the petals, like jewels that entwine.
In a world turned to crystal, dreams softly gleam,
Frosted fantasies waken, as if from a dream.

A breath of the morning, so crisp and so clear,
Each whisper of nature, a song to the ear.
Life stirs in the silence, the hush of the glow,
Wrapping the earth in a delicate show.

Nature's embrace, in a blanket of white,
Each flake tells a story, a moment of light.
Footsteps leave traces on this canvas so pure,
In frost's gentle cradle, our spirits endure.

The sun peeks above, with a warm, golden hue,
Melting away shadows, revealing the true.
Frosted fantasies dance in the warmth of the rays,
Awakening hearts to the beauty of days.

So let us venture forth, in this magical realm,
Where dreams find their harbor, and thoughts overwhelm.
Frosted enchantments await with each breath,
In this blissful embrace, we conquer our depth.

Chasing the Glint of Night

With every step forward, the stars start to glow,
Guiding our journey, with a soft, secret flow.
Chasing the glint of the night's endless maze,
Lost in the wonder, as time gently sways.

Whispers of shadows weave tales through the air,
Mysteries beckon from beyond with a flare.
In the twilight's whisper, our dreams take their flight,
Chasing the glint of the shimmering night.

The moon casts its glow on the path that we tread,
Painting our hopes, like the words left unsaid.
Every twinkle above tells a story of old,
As we chase the glimmer, our spirits unfold.

Moments suspended in the velvet-like space,
Each heartbeat a compass, leading to grace.
Waltzing with dreams that drift close in their flight,
Embracing the magic while chasing the night.

So let us be wanderers, hearts open wide,
Together we'll journey, with stars as our guide.
As we chase the glint, let our souls take to flight,
In the embrace of the dark, we'll find our true light.

Against the Frosty Veil

Whispers of winter cling in cold, silent air,
Wrapped in a shroud, the world feels so bare.
Against the frosty veil, the heart starts to thrum,
Yearning for warmth, through the silence we come.

Branches stand still, dressed in crystalline lace,
Nature's own artwork, a delicate grace.
In the stillness, each breath turns to mist,
In this frozen expanse, there's warmth in the twist.

The crackle of frost underfoot as we tread,
With each step we take, new paths to be led.
Promises linger in the chill we despise,
But beauty emerges as the heart opens wide.

The glow of the fire contrasts the frost, bright,
As shadows dance lightly, giving warmth to the night.
Against the frosty veil, we find our own way,
In the heart of the cold, there's live in the fray.

So let us embrace what the frost might conceal,
Finding the warmth in the cool, tangible feel.
In the hush of the cold, where dreams intertwine,
Against the frosty veil, our spirits will shine.

Silver Veils of Quietude

In the soft light of the dawn,
Whispers weave through the trees.
Silence drapes a gentle shawl,
Comfort rests on the breeze.

Beneath the weight of morning dew,
Silver veils hang low and sweet.
Nature hums a lullaby,
In harmony, all hearts meet.

Echoes dance in stillness found,
Softly cradled by the day.
Time unfolds in quiet grace,
As shadows gently sway.

Moments linger, close and dear,
Wrapped in layers of the night.
Every breath, a sacred tone,
In the grasp of warming light.

Magic stirs beneath the trees,
In this realm of calm delight.
Silver veils of quietude,
Embrace the coming flight.

A Chilling Lullaby

Beneath the moon's watchful eye,
Whispers chase the evening's breath.
A chilling lullaby begins,
Serenade of silent death.

Frost-kissed dreams drift in the air,
Hushed tones cradle night's embrace.
Stars flicker, twinkling echoes,
In this dark, enchanted space.

Gentle shivers cross the skin,
As shadows play their soft refrain.
Melodies of chilly winds,
Stir the heart beneath the pain.

Time slows down and holds its breath,
As night unravels found delights.
Cradled in the arms of dusk,
Hope awakens with the lights.

A lullaby that chills the bones,
Yet warms the depths of every soul.
In the night, we find our truth,
In darkness, love makes us whole.

Secrets in the Frost-kissed Air

In the hush of early morn,
Frost-kissed whispers softly sigh.
Secrets hide in every flake,
Glimmers twinkle in the sky.

Nature guards her hidden tales,
Wrapped in layers of icy light.
Each breath a story, softly told,
In the quiet veil of night.

Branches cradle fragile dreams,
Halos glisten, secrets bare.
In this chill, the heart reveals,
Hopes entwined in frosty air.

Every shiver, every breath,
Carries tales of love and loss.
Underneath the gleaming frost,
Lies the weight of every cross.

Embrace the quiet, hold it close,
Let the chill caress your heart.
For in the frost, a spark ignites,
A new beginning, a fresh start.

Glimmers of Gossamer Light

In the break of golden dawn,
Glimmers dance on dew-kissed leaves.
Moments flicker, soft and bright,
Entwined in nature's gentle weaves.

Gossamer threads weave through the trees,
Whispers twirl in morning's grace.
As sunlight spills across the land,
Life awakens in each face.

Every ray a tender touch,
Drawing hearts to pause and feel.
In the warmth, the world unfolds,
Time reveals its wondrous wheel.

Shadows stretch and join the play,
As colors burst from night's retreat.
In this moment, pure and still,
Life dances on with joy complete.

Glimmers spark hope in our days,
Reminding us there's magic here.
In the light, let spirits soar,
And embrace each dawning cheer.

Frosted Glories Under the Starlit Sky

Beneath the stars, the world aglow,
Frosted glories dance, whispers flow.
Moonlit silver on leaves does gleam,
Night's sweet magic, a silent dream.

Crystals form like nature's lace,
Softly falling, time slows its pace.
Voices echo in the chill,
Embracing warmth as the night stands still.

With each breath, the air turns bright,
Sparkles twinkle, a wondrous sight.
Underneath the starlit dome,
Hearts awaken, far from home.

Glimmers of hope amidst the dark,
Frosted glories leave their mark.
In every flake, a story told,
Whispers of magic, tender and bold.

As dawn approaches, the frost will fade,
Yet in memories, it will not jade.
Under the stars, forever we'll keep,
Frosted glories in dreams we leap.

Illuminous Frost and Night's Veil

A veil of night wraps the earth so tight,
Illuminous frost paints the world in white.
Silvery shadows dance in the moon,
Singing soft songs, a gentle tune.

Each breath of cold, a misty sigh,
Stars above twinkle in the sky.
Frost-kissed whispers through branches creep,
In the stillness, the secrets we keep.

Under the gaze of the watchful night,
The frost unveils a hidden light.
Softly glowing on every surface,
Nature's art, a serene purpose.

With every step, the crunch is clear,
Illuminous paths, the heart draws near.
Wrapped in chilly, starlit grace,
Embracing the quiet, a warm embrace.

As night wanes, colors start to blend,
Illuminous frost, a fleeting friend.
Yet in our hearts, it shall remain,
A night of wonders, forever gain.

Ethereal Chill of the Still Night

Ethereal chill blankets the ground,
In the still night, a silence profound.
Snowflakes swirl like spirits free,
Whispers of dreams in harmony.

The moon hangs low in the velvet sky,
Casting shadows as time drifts by.
Frosted breath in the frosty air,
Moments of magic linger everywhere.

Silent woods wrapped in silver sheen,
Glimmers of beauty, a celestial scene.
Softly twinkling, the stars take flight,
A tapestry woven of sheer delight.

Each heartbeat echoes, a rhythmic sound,
In the embrace of the night unbound.
Ethereal chill, a sacred pause,
In nature's stillness, we find our cause.

As dawn approaches with soft, golden hues,
We cherish the night, its quiet muse.
Memories tucked in the folds of light,
Ethereal chill, our guiding sight.

Celestial Threads on Icy Paths

Celestial threads weave through the trees,
Icy paths whisper with the breeze.
Frosted patterns trace nature's hand,
Crafted wonder across the land.

Stars above shimmer with righteous glow,
While the earth below wears a blanket of snow.
Each step we take, a story unfolds,
Tales of the night in silver and gold.

Moonlit shadows dance with grace,
In this dreamlike, enchanted space.
Celestial spirits guide our way,
Through icy paths, we shall sway.

With every breath, the magic grows,
On these threads, our adventure flows.
Whispers of warmth in the frosty air,
A tapestry woven with love and care.

As daylight breaks and shadows flee,
Celestial threads we still can see.
In our hearts, they gently remain,
Icy paths lead us home again.

Nighttime's Diamond-coated Boughs

Underneath the starlit skies,
Branches glisten, shimmering guise.
Each droplet holds a tale untold,
Nature's magic, pure and bold.

Silent whispers in the air,
Moonlight dances without care.
Beneath the weight of winter's grace,
Dreams unfold in quiet space.

A canvas of the darkest night,
Adorned with gems, a breathtaking sight.
Each flicker in the frigid air,
A world transformed, beyond compare.

Frosted leaves with secrets keep,
In the silence, stars do seep.
Gentle winds weave stories near,
As nighttime whispers, crystal-clear.

Underneath the diamond boughs,
Where nature breathes and beauty bows.
A moment caught in endless time,
Nighttime's splendor, pure and prime.

A Flicker of Light in Darkness

In the depth of shadow's clutch,
A spark ignites, it means so much.
Like a candle in the night,
Hope emerges, shining bright.

Whispers travel on the breeze,
Softly spoken, urging ease.
Every heart can find its way,
Guided through the night and fray.

Stars awake, they twinkle high,
Painting dreams across the sky.
One small flame, a mighty fight,
Lighting paths with pure delight.

Glimmers cast on faces fair,
A reminder of love's care.
Turning dark to golden hues,
Life awakens with fresh views.

A flicker holds a universe,
In the silence, hear the verse.
Even shadows need a spark,
Hope arrives, igniting dark.

Crystalline Nightfall

Whispers of the night are near,
As darkness wraps the world, sincere.
In crystalline shrouds, it softly glows,
Magic stirs where the night wind blows.

Each icy flake a story spun,
Under the gaze of the rising sun.
A tapestry of stars unfurled,
Painting dreams upon the world.

Silver beams on fallen snow,
Capturing all that comes and goes.
Moonlight weaves a silken thread,
Binding all, where dreams are fed.

Frozen whispers in the night,
Kissing shadows with sheer light.
Harmony in cold embrace,
Nights adorned with timeless grace.

Crystalline dreams, they softly blend,
Where the night and light suspend.
A fleeting charm, a quiet call,
Embracing hearts in nightfall's thrall.

Whispers of Chill and Light

Beneath the whispering trees,
The chill dances on cool breeze.
Light flickers like a distant star,
A gentle touch, though near and far.

Each breath is crisp, the earth aglow,
As twilight paints the land below.
Embers fade, but hope's alight,
In the stillness of the night.

Crickets sing their evening tune,
While shadows play with waning moon.
Every moment glimmers bright,
In the garment of soft light.

A lantern's glow, a warm embrace,
Invites the heart to find its place.
Whispers chatter under skies,
In tranquility, peace lies.

Holding warmth in fingers tight,
While the chill invites the night.
In this dance, both light and dark,
Whispers breathe their sacred mark.

Shining Through the Stillness

In twilight's tender embrace,
Light breaks the night's cold face.
Whispers dance on gentle air,
Dreams awaken, everywhere.

Silent echoes softly play,
The dawn will greet the day.
Stars flicker in the blue,
There's magic in the view.

Moonlight paints the world so bright,
Guiding paths through the night.
Hope that trickles like a stream,
Rising like a waking dream.

Beneath the sky's vast dome,
Hearts find their way back home.
Through the stillness, we will find,
Peace that soothes and warms the mind.

Every moment holds its worth,
In the quiet of the earth.
Together, we'll embrace the light,
Shining through the heart of night.

Ghosts of Winter's Glow

Frosted whispers fill the air,
Ghosts of winter gently stare.
Beneath the snow, a tale unfolds,
Of warmth remembered, love retold.

Lights flicker in the distant glow,
With every step, soft shadows flow.
In the silence, spirits wake,
Guarding the dreams that we make.

Time stands still in the frigid night,
Every star a guiding light.
Stories linger, soft and sweet,
In the winter's quiet beat.

Crystalline trees reach for the sky,
Embracing the long, slow sigh.
Echoes wrap like a warm shawl,
Comfort found in the still fall.

As darkness melts to morning's hue,
The ghosts whisper, "We're here for you."
Together we'll walk, hand in hand,
In winter's glow, we'll bravely stand.

Enchantment in the Ice

Crystals form in the late dawn,
A world reborn, a new song.
In frozen realms, dreams softly glide,
Where hearts and hopes do abide.

Every flake tells a story old,
Of warmth within the bitter cold.
Glistening paths that weave and sway,
Through twilight's blush, in soft decay.

The air is thick with magic's spark,
As daylight dances through the dark.
With every step on winter's lace,
We find enchantment, a sacred space.

Beneath the veil of icy blue,
Life's secrets beckon, bold and true.
Timeless beauty, calm and bright,
In the heart, winter ignites.

So here we stand, in awe we gaze,
At nature's pure, enchanting maze.
With every breath, alive we feel,
The magic in the world that's real.

Starlit Whispers in the Cold

Underneath the starry skies,
Whispers float where silence lies.
Cold winds carry tales of old,
Secrets wrapped in stories told.

Glimmers dance on frosty ground,
In the hush, a peace is found.
Moonbeams spill like silver wine,
Illuminating paths that shine.

Every heartbeat syncs with night,
Drawn to the cosmic light.
With every breath, the chill we share,
Echoes of love linger in the air.

Time unfolds in velvet night,
Stars are guides, pure and bright.
Together, beneath the cold embrace,
We find our place, our sacred space.

In starlit whispers, hearts ignite,
Filling shadows with our light.
Through the silence, we will stay,
Finding magic in the gray.

A Tapestry of Glazed Wonder

In the morning's gentle glow,
Colors dance in soft embrace,
Threads of gold and deep cerulean,
Weaving dreams in silent space.

Whispers of the vibrant hue,
Tell of places yet to find,
Every stitch a tale anew,
Binding heart and soul entwined.

Beneath the arch of azure skies,
Nature sings a painted song,
With every brush, the spirit flies,
In this world, we all belong.

The tapestry of joy unfurls,
Each layer tells a story bright,
Innocence in swirls and twirls,
A treasure in the soft twilight.

So let us wander hand in hand,
Through fields of woven grace and cheer,
In this tapestry, we stand,
In the love that brings us near.

Shards of Light in Winter's Hold

Crystals glisten on the trees,
Nature's breath, a frozen sigh,
Each ray breaks through winter's freeze,
Painting shadows on the sky.

Footsteps crunch on snowy ground,
Echoes travel through still night,
In the cold, the warmth is found,
A flicker sparks, a silver light.

As stars twinkle, memories glow,
The heart whispers in the cold,
Every flake a tale to show,
In the quiet, stories unfold.

Veils of mist, a magic thread,
Connecting souls in soft embrace,
While dreams awaken from their bed,
In winter's chill, we find our place.

With each dawn, the shards ignite,
A canvas painted by the dawn,
In the cradle of the night,
Hope emerges, new day drawn.

Nightfall's Ethereal Touch

As dusk descends on whispered hills,
Stars awaken, shy and bright,
In the twilight, soft time stills,
Painting dreams in silver light.

Moonlight dances on the sea,
Casting shadows, calm and deep,
A gentle whisper calls to me,
In the embrace of night, I sleep.

Crickets sing a lullaby,
Nature's pulse, a soothing beat,
While the world begins to sigh,
In the dark, all hearts can meet.

Veils of clouds, a silken shroud,
Wrap the earth in tender care,
In this space, I stand unbowed,
Finding solace, peace laid bare.

Each moment holds a breathless pause,
As constellations weave their tales,
Under night's enchanting laws,
In stillness, every spirit sails.

Glistening Waltz of Shadows

In the twilight, shadows play,
Silhouettes in graceful dance,
Every corner, shades at bay,
Whirling in a soft romance.

Moonbeams weave a silver thread,
Across the floor of night's embrace,
In this dance, the heart is led,
Lost in rhythm, found in grace.

Each hush speaks of dreams untold,
As darkness swirls with starlit gleam,
Here, the secrets gently unfold,
In the waltz, we follow the dream.

With every step, the spirits soar,
Glistening in the night's pure glow,
In the dance, we're evermore,
In the shadows, love will flow.

So take my hand, we'll twirl and spin,
In the magic, we will find,
Together, let the night begin,
In this waltz, our hearts aligned.

Shades of Night on a Frosty Canvas

On a frosty canvas, shadows play,
Whispers of winter drift and sway.
Stars sprinkle silver across the dark,
While silent winds leave their mark.

The moon hangs low, a glowing pearl,
Casting dreams in a silent whirl.
Branches shimmer with glistening dew,
In the stillness, everything feels new.

Echoes of night weave a soft tune,
Beneath a watchful, ancient moon.
The chill wraps tight like a velvet cloak,
In the depths of night, hearts provoke.

Colors fade as black takes hold,
Embracing the tales that night has told.
Each breath of cold a gentle sigh,
Cradling secrets as time slips by.

In this realm where dreams ignite,
Shades dance softly, pure and light.
Every glance a fleeting chance,
In the dark, we find our romance.

Twilight's Brilliant Touch

Beneath the folds of twilight's hue,
Soft whispers rise in the cool, damp dew.
Golden rays mingle with shadows deep,
As the world prepares for restful sleep.

Mountains stand tall in a purple blaze,
Capturing the last light's warm gaze.
Birds settle down in the brambles tight,
While day surrenders to the approaching night.

The horizon burns with a fiery kiss,
A moment's beauty we cannot miss.
Time seems to slow, wrapped in gold,
As stories of dusk begin to unfold.

The sky's palette, a wondrous painting,
In vivid strokes, our hearts gaining.
Each color shifts, a fleeting dance,
Inviting us all to take a chance.

And as the stars begin to ignite,
We cherish the magic of the twilight light.
In these moments, life feels right,
Embraced by the warmth of the coming night.

Dancing Splinters of Light

Along the path, the shadows flit,
Dancing splinters of light brightly knit.
Sunbeams weave through branches bare,
Enveloping the world in golden air.

Each ray a whisper, soft and sweet,
Tapping the heart with a gentle beat.
Nature twirls in jubilant grace,
In the sunlight's embrace, all find their place.

Leaves shimmer like diamonds, crisp and bright,
In the embrace of the morning light.
Colors collide in a lively dance,
Inviting each soul to take a chance.

Moments gleam, time slows down,
In the vibrance, we wear a crown.
Every flicker a story shared,
In the splendor of light, we are bared.

As shadows stretch and daylight fades,
We hold close the warmth that never parades.
Dancing splinters, a vivid blend,
Whispering secrets that never end.

Icy Veils and Luminous Tales

Icy veils drape the silent ground,
Whispering softly, without a sound.
Frosty breath curls in the chilly air,
Painting stories beyond compare.

In the moonlight, crystals glimmer bright,
Weaving luminous tales in the night.
Nature, adorned in white and blue,
Embraces beauty, ever true.

Frozen whispers echo near and far,
Each drop of ice, a fallen star.
The world transformed, a tranquil sight,
Wrapped in serenity, pure delight.

With each step, the crunch of frost,
In this stillness, no joy is lost.
Every glance reveals a hidden grace,
In icy veils, we find our place.

As dawn breaks forth, the sun will rise,
Warming hearts and clearing skies.
Yet even then, the tales remain,
In icy veils, there's beauty and gain.

Velvet Night

The sky drapes low, a velvet shroud,
Stars blink softly, wrapped in cloud.
Silent whispers weave through the trees,
In this calm embrace, the heart finds ease.

Moonlight spills like silver wine,
Crickets sing in a gentle line.
Dreams take flight on wings of night,
In the stillness, shadows ignite.

The world fades under the dark embrace,
Only the night holds a gentle grace.
A tapestry woven with starlit thread,
In velvet whispers, all fears are shed.

Hushed are the secrets long kept within,
Each breath a promise, each heartbeat a win.
Mysteries gather where darkness clings,
As the night softly hums and sings.

Rest now, dear soul, in this soothing view,
Let the velvet night comfort you.
For in the silence, solace flows,
A tranquil haven where peace bestows.

When dawn creeps in, the dreams take flight,
In the arms of night, there's pure delight.
Hold on to whispers, let them take flight,
For every ending brings new light.

Glittering Whispers

In twilight's glow, the stars awake,
A dance of lights on the shimmering lake.
Whispers of magic float on the breeze,
A serenade sung by rustling leaves.

Each glittering gem in the sky above,
Tells tales of dreams, of wonder, of love.
A flicker of hope in the evening's calm,
An echo of warmth, a soothing balm.

The night unfolds its sparkling gown,
While shadows play on the edges of town.
Every twinkle tells a story untold,
In the silence where mysteries unfold.

With every breath, the whispers grow bright,
A symphony born out of pure night.
Catch the laughter that dances so free,
In every star, a memory.

Let the glittering whispers guide your way,
Through the corridors of night and day.
For in every flicker, there's light and grace,
A reminder to cherish this beautiful place.

As dawn approaches, the whispers will fade,
But in your heart, their magic won't jade.
Hold onto the glimmer, let it shine through,
For every whisper is a part of you.

The Hush of Silvered Air

In the hush of the night, the world stands still,
A tranquil moment, a gentle thrill.
Silvered air whispers secrets untold,
Wrapped in the silence, mysteries unfold.

Stars twinkle softly, a celestial glow,
Guiding lost hearts where dreams can flow.
Moonbeams dance on the velvet sea,
In the hush of air, there's pure serenity.

The night is a canvas, painted with light,
In every shadow, a story takes flight.
Silence holds treasures too rare to measure,
In the heart of the hush, we find our treasure.

Feel the stillness wrap around like a cloak,
A soft serenade that the night has spoke.
Every breath a testament to dreams that dare,
In the stillness, we find hope laid bare.

As morning beckons with golden hues,
The hush of silvered air softly renews.
In every dawn that breaks the night's tether,
Lives the promise of new adventures together.

So cherish the moment, the soft repose,
For in the hush, the beauty grows.
A reminder that even in silence, we share,
The whispering love of the silvered air.

When Ice Meets the Glow

In winter's chill, where shadows stretch wide,
The world lies still, a frosted pride.
Ice crystals shimmer, reflect the light,
When ice meets the glow, it sparkles bright.

Each breath a mist, a fleeting sigh,
Painting the air with dreams that fly.
The dawn breaks soft, a tender embrace,
As warmth awakens the frozen space.

Branches bow low, heavy with grace,
Nature whispers in this quiet place.
A symphony plays in the stillness so grand,
As ice dances gently at winter's command.

The light flickers softly on each crystal sphere,
Transforming the cold, exposing the cheer.
When ice meets the glow, a miracle shows,
How beauty can flourish in deep winter's throes.

Hold close the warmth, let the heartbeat ignite,
As shadows retreat, embracing the light.
For every cold moment will soon meet the thaw,
In the arms of the glow, we find our awe.

So wander through winters with eyes open wide,
When ice meets the glow, let your spirit glide.
For magic awaits where the seasons will roam,
In nature's embrace, we find our home.

Enigmatic Blush of Winter

In the dusky light, a blush spills fair,
The enigmatic whispers drift through the air.
Winter's breath carries secrets profound,
In every corner where silence is found.

Shadows lengthen, draped in white,
The world a wonder, a mystical sight.
Frost-kissed petals, a delicate hue,
Unraveled beauty in every view.

The landscape glows with a gentle grace,
Winter's embrace, a soft, warm lace.
Crimson and gold spark beneath the frost,
In the blush of winter, nothing is lost.

Every snowfall is a canvas divine,
Etching stories that intertwine.
Each flake a whisper, unique in its flight,
Painting the world in pure delight.

As twilight settles, the blush deepens more,
A promise of warmth behind winter's door.
In this mystique, find solace and cheer,
For the enigmatic blush will always draw near.

Embrace the chill, the beauty it brings,
In winter's hush, the heart sings.
For in every moment, where cold meets the light,
Lives the enchanting blush of winter, so bright.

www.ingramcontent.com/pod-product-compliance
Ingram Content Group UK Ltd.
Pitfield, Milton Keynes, MK11 3LW, UK
UKHW031940151224
452382UK00006B/229